MOTIVES
OF THE
HEART

A BIBLICAL STUDY IN
PRIDE AND HUMILITY

REB BRADLEY

FAMILY MINISTRIES PUBLISHING
Sheridan, California

FAMILY MINISTRIES PUBLISHING
PO Box 266
Sheridan, California 95681
www.familyministries.com

Prepared as a syllabus for the leadership
training seminar Motives of the Heart

All Bible quotes:
New International version,
unless otherwise stated

Motives of the Heart

HOW DOES GOD VIEW PRIDE?

*Proverbs 21:4 **Haughty eyes and a proud heart**, the lamp of the wicked, **are sin!***

*1 Samuel 15:23 For rebellion is like the sin of divination, and arrogance **like the evil of idolatry.** Because you have rejected the word of the LORD, he has rejected you as king."*

*Proverbs 6:16 There are six things **the LORD hates**, seven that are **detestable** to him: 17 haughty eyes, a lying tongue, hands that shed innocent blood,*

*Job 41:34 **He looks down** on all that are haughty; he is king over all that are proud."*

*Psalms 101:5 Whoever slanders his neighbor in secret, him will I put to silence; whoever has haughty eyes and a proud heart, him will **I not endure.***

*Psalms 138:6 Though the LORD is on high, he looks upon the lowly, but the proud **he knows from afar.***

*Proverbs 3:34 **He mocks proud mockers** but gives grace to the humble.*

*Proverbs 8:13 To fear the LORD is to hate evil; **I hate pride and arrogance,** evil behavior and perverse speech.*

1 Corinthians 1:28   He chose the lowly things of this world and the despised things--and the things that are not--to nullify the things that are, 29 so that **no one may boast before him.**

Ephesians 2:9   not by works, **so that no one can boast.**

Psalms 5:5   The arrogant **cannot stand in your presence; you hate** *all who do wrong.*

Proverbs 16:5 **The LORD detests all the proud of heart.** *Be sure of this: They* **will not go unpunished.**

HOW DOES GOD VIEW HUMILITY?

Colossians 3:12   Therefore, as God's chosen people, holy and dearly loved, **clothe yourselves with** *compassion, kindness,* **humility,** *gentleness and patience.*

Titus 3:2   to slander no one, to be peaceable and considerate, and to **show true humility toward all men.**

James 4:10 **Humble yourselves before the Lord,** *and he will lift you up.*

1 Peter 3:8   Finally, all of you, live in harmony with one another; be sympathetic, love as brothers, **be compassionate and humble.**

1 Peter 5:5 Young men, in the same way be submissive to those who are older. All of you, **clothe yourselves with humility toward one another, because, "God opposes the proud but gives grace to the humble."**

WHEN DOES JUDGMENT COME UPON THE PROUD?

James 4:6 But he gives us more grace. That is why Scripture says: "God **opposes the proud** *but gives grace to the humble."*

2 Chronicles 32:25 But Hezekiah's heart was proud and he did not respond to the kindness shown him; **therefore the Lord's wrath was on him** *and on Judah and Jerusalem. 26 Then Hezekiah repented of the pride of his heart, as did the people of Jerusalem; therefore the Lord's wrath did not come upon them during the days of Hezekiah.*

Daniel 4:37 Now I, Nebuchadnezzar, praise and exalt and glorify the King of heaven, because everything he does is right and all his ways are just. And those who walk in pride **he is able to humble.**

2 Chronicles 26:16 But after Uzziah became powerful, **his pride led to his downfall.** *He was unfaithful to the LORD his God, and entered the temple of the LORD to burn incense on the altar of incense.*

Luke 1:51 He has performed mighty deeds with his arm; **he has scattered** *those who are proud in their* *inmost thoughts. 52* **He has brought down** *rulers from their thrones but has lifted up the humble.*

Proverbs 16:18 **Pride goes before destruction**, *a haughty spirit* **before a fall.**

Proverbs 18:12 **Before his downfall a man's heart is proud**, *but humility comes before honor.*

Isaiah 2:11 The eyes of the arrogant man **will be humbled** *and the pride of men* **brought low;** *the LORD alone will be exalted in that day. 12 The LORD Almighty has* **a day in store** *for all the proud and lofty, for all that is exalted (and* **they will be humbled),**

Isaiah 2:17 The arrogance of man **will be brought low** *and the pride of men* **humbled;** *the LORD alone will be exalted in that day,*

Isaiah 13:11 I will punish the world for its evil, the wicked for their sins. **I will put an end** *to the arrogance of the haughty and* **will humble the pride of the ruthless**. *(Proverbs 15:25)*

Isaiah 25:11 They will spread out their hands in it, as a swimmer spreads out his hands to swim. God **will bring down their pride** *despite the cleverness of their hands. (Isaiah 23:9)*

Jeremiah 49:16 The terror you inspire and the pride of your heart have deceived you, you who live in the clefts of the rocks, who occupy the heights of the hill. Though you build your nest as high as the

*eagle's, from there **I will bring you down,***" declares
the LORD. (Psalms 18:27; Isaiah 5:15)

*Matthew 23:12   For whoever exalts himself **will be***
***humbled**, and whoever humbles himself will be
exalted.

*Luke 14:8   "When someone invites you to a wedding
*feast, do not take the place of honor, for a person
*more distinguished than you may have been invited.
*9 If so, the host who invited both of you will come
*and say to you, 'Give this man your seat.' Then,
*humiliated, you will have to take the least important
*place. 10 But when you are invited, take the lowest
*place, so that when your host comes, he will say to
*you, 'Friend, move up to a better place.' Then you
*will be honored in the presence of all your fellow
*guests. 11 For **everyone who exalts himself will be***
***humbled**, and he who humbles himself will be
exalted."

*Luke 18:14   "I tell you that this man, rather than the
*other, went home justified before God. For **everyone***
***who exalts himself will be humbled**, and he who
humbles himself will be exalted."

DEFINING PRIDE AND HUMILITY

DEFINITIONS:

Pride is an over-exalted view of one's own importance. It is excessive self-concern.

Hebrew
ge'ah, gay-aw'; from gaah, to mount up; arrogance

Greek
phusioo, foo-see-o'-o; growth by germination or expansion; sense of blowing; to inflate, puff up

huperephanos, hoop-er-ay'-fan-os; appearing above others (conspicuous), i.e. (fig.) haughty

Humility is regarding oneself as unimportant. It is selflessness. (Seeing yourself as God sees you.)

Hebrew: *forced to bow down*

shachah, shaw-khaw'; a prim. root; to depress, i.e. prostrate (espec. reflex. in homage to royalty or God):--bow (self) down, crouch, fall down (flat), humbly beseech, do (make) obeisance, do reverence, make to stoop, worship.

shaphel, shaw-fale'; a prim. root; to depress or sink (espec. fig. to humiliate, intrans. or trans.):--abase, bring (cast, put) down, debase, humble (self), be (bring, lay, make, put) low (-er).

shephal, (Chald.), shef-al'; abase, humble, put down, subdue.

raphac, raw-fas'; a prim. root; to trample, i.e. prostrate:--humble self, submit self.

'anavah, an-aw-vaw'; condescension, human and subj. (modesty), or divine and obj. (clemency):--gentleness, humility, meekness.

daka', daw-kaw'; a prim. root - to crumble; trans. to bruise (lit. or fig.): beat to pieces, break (in pieces), bruise, contrite, crush, destroy, humble, oppress, smite.

shuwach, shoo'-akh; a prim. root; to sink, lit. or fig.:--bow down, incline, humble.

tsana', tsaw-nah'; a prim. root; to humiliate:-- humbly, lowly.

Greek
tapeinos, tap-i-nos; lowliness or humility of mind, i.e. modesty: feeling cast down;

PRIDE IS SELF LOVE

1. PRIDE IS SELF-CONSUMED

2 Timothy 3:2   People will be lovers of themselves, lovers of money, boastful, proud, abusive, disobedient to their parents, ungrateful, unholy,

Mat 22:39 And the second is like it: 'Love your neighbor as yourself.'

• Pride is self-preoccupation. It interprets life in light of its own interests.

• Pride considers himself so important that he stays on his own mind all day long.

• Pride is vain. He looks in the mirror and says, "I like what I see."

HUMILITY IS SELFLESSNESS

1. HUMILITY IS CONSUMED WITH GOD AND OTHERS

Mat 16:24 Then Jesus said to his disciples, "If anyone would come after me, he must deny himself and take up his cross and follow me.

• Humility doesn't think badly of himself. He doesn't think of himself.

• Humility doesn't hate what he sees in the mirror. He finds it unimportant to look in the mirror.

PRIDE IS SELF LOVE

2. PRIDE HATES ITSELF

*Eph 5:29 After all, no one ever hated his own body, but
he feeds and cares for it, just as Christ does the church*

*Col 2:18 Do not let anyone who delights in false
humility and the worship of angels disqualify you for the
prize. Such a person goes into great detail about what
he has seen, and his unspiritual mind puffs him up with
idle notions., 23 Such regulations indeed have an
appearance of wisdom, with their self-imposed worship,
their false humility and their harsh treatment of the
body, but they lack any value in restraining sensual
indulgence.*

• Pride is vain. He looks in the mirror and says,
"I hate what I see."

• Pride perceives "self-hate" as excessive
humility, but it is only because he cares so
much about himself that he feels such anger.
He is mad at himself for letting himself down. It
is excessive self-concern that produces
self-hate.

• Pride glories in its self-hate.

• Pride refuses to submit to forgiveness. He
demands to atone for his own sins.

HUMILITY IS SELFLESSNESS

2. HUMILITY ESTEEMS OTHERS HIGHLY

Philippians 2:3   Do nothing out of selfish ambition or vain conceit, but in humility consider others better than yourselves. 5   Your attitude should be the same as that of Christ Jesus: 6 Who, being in very nature God, did not consider equality with God something to be grasped, 7 but made himself nothing, taking the very nature of a servant, being made in human likeness. 8 And being found in appearance as a man, he humbled himself and became obedient to death-- even death on a cross! 9 Therefore God exalted him to the highest place and gave him the name that is above every name,

• Humility doesn't perceive himself as less important than others. He simply treats others as more important than himself.

PRIDE IS SELF LOVE

3. PRIDE IS DEBILITATING

• Pride cares so much for himself that he is ineffective in caring for others.

• Pride is consumed with himself and what he wants. He tends to his own needs before others.

• Pride may be consumed with meeting others needs, but does so for self-centered reasons, ie: self-esteem, approval, popularity, etc.

HUMILITY IS SELFLESSNESS

3. HUMILITY IS FREE TO LOVE OTHERS

1 Corinthians 13:5 It is not rude, it is not self-seeking, it is not easily angered, it keeps no record of wrongs.

• Humility is unhampered by self-preoccupation, so naturally and easily thinks of others first.

• Humility is personally unfazed by a lack of deserved appreciation or respect from others.

PRIDE IS INSECURE

1. PRIDE IS DEFENSIVE

Proverbs 9:8 Do not rebuke a mocker or he will hate you; rebuke a wise man and he will love you.

Proverbs 12:1 Whoever loves discipline loves knowledge, but he who hates correction is stupid.

Proverbs 12:15 The way of a fool seems right to him, but a wise man listens to advice.

Proverbs 17:9 He who covers over an offense promotes love, but whoever repeats the matter separates close friends.

Proverbs 28:13 He who conceals his sins does not prosper, but whoever confesses and renounces them finds mercy.

Proverbs 10:12 Hatred stirs up dissension, but love covers over all wrongs.

Job 40:8 "Would you discredit my justice? Would you condemn me to justify yourself?

• Pride has a fragile self-concept.

• Pride can be easily hurt or offended. Self-concept is easily threatened and must be defended.

• Pride is not open to criticism. It's very defensive and seeks to "save face." It doesn't want to believe it's at fault. It can be easily angered.

• Pride isn't very teachable. It doesn't desire to be open.

• Pride always justifies its actions to those who question.

• Pride is always right and finds fault with the reprover.

• Pride will rely on any number of defense mechanisms to avoid accepting personal responsibility.

• Pride finds reason to disregard any criticism. It challenge the credibility of the reprover.

• Pride doesn't accept responsibility for his actions, and may try to make others feel guilty for his mistakes.

• Pride hates to admit fault. It is difficult for him to say, "I'm sorry. Please forgive me."

HUMILITY IS SECURE

1. HUMILITY LOVES CORRECTION

Proverbs 9:8 Do not rebuke a mocker or he will hate you; rebuke a wise man and he will love you. 9 Instruct a wise man and he will be wiser still; teach a righteous man and he will add to his learning.

Proverbs 12:1 Whoever loves discipline loves knowledge, but he who hates correction is stupid.

Proverbs 12:15 The way of a fool seems right to him, but a wise man listens to advice.

Proverbs 19:25 Flog a mocker, and the simple will learn prudence; rebuke a discerning man, and he will gain knowledge.

• Humility is sure of who he is before the Lord. He doesn't need others approval.

• Humility has a clear conscience before the Lord. It is not defensive and does not get hurt very easily.

• Humility recognizes his own imperfections, so is open to and desirous of reproof or knowledge from any source. (That is, anything congruent with the word of God.)

• Humility is very understanding and isn't easily antagonized.

• Humility is very loving.

PRIDE IS INSECURE

2. PRIDE CONTROLS

Proverbs 11:2 When pride comes, then comes disgrace, but with humility comes wisdom.

Proverbs 17:7 Arrogant lips are unsuited to a fool-- how much worse lying lips to a ruler!

Ezekiel 28:17 Your heart became proud on account of your beauty, and you corrupted your wisdom because of your splendor. So I threw you to the earth; I made a spectacle of you before kings.

James 3:14-16 But if you harbor bitter envy and selfish ambition in your hearts, do not boast about it or deny the truth. 15 Such "wisdom" does not come down from heaven but is earthly, unspiritual, of the devil. 16 For where you have envy and selfish ambition, there you find disorder and every evil practice.

• Pride controls you. It actually blinds you to itself. It filters everything you perceive. It clouds your thinking. It is the attitude that spawns your responses.

• Pride is so defensive that he thinks that this list of symptoms does not apply to him. In fact, pride will read a list like this and immediately say, "So-and so sure needs to read this!"

• Pride is so determined to resist conviction that he will search for every conceivable reason to discredit this symptom list.

• Pride is rooted in foolishness

HUMILITY IS SECURE

2. HUMILITY IS SELF-CONTROLLED

1 Corinthians 13:12 Now we see but a poor reflection as in a mirror; then we shall see face to face. Now I know in part; then I shall know fully, even as I am fully known.

James 3:13 Who is wise and understanding among you? Let him show it by his good life, by deeds done in the humility that comes from wisdom. 17 But the wisdom that comes from heaven is first of all pure; then peace-loving, considerate, submissive, full of mercy and good fruit, impartial and sincere.

Proverbs 11:2 When pride comes, then comes disgrace, but with humility comes wisdom.

Proverbs 13:10 Pride only breeds quarrels, but wisdom is found in those who take advice.

Proverbs 15:33 The fear of the LORD teaches a man wisdom, and humility comes before honor.

- Humility thinks clearly.

- Humility knows it has blind spots.

- Humility is not constrained by passions so is able to make decisions unhampered by the carnal nature.

- Humility is an outgrowth of wisdom.

PRIDE ASPIRES TO BE GREAT!

1. PRIDE LOVES TO BE HONORED

Proverbs 25:6-7 Do not exalt yourself in the king's presence, and do not claim a place among great men; 7 it is better for him to say to you, "Come up here," than for him to humiliate you before a nobleman. What you have seen with your eyes 27 It is not good to eat too much honey, nor is it honorable to seek one's own honor.

3 John 1:9 I wrote to the church, but Diotrephes, who loves to be first, will have nothing to do with us.

• He values greatly his reputation. It's hard for pride to be a nobody.

• Pride loves a title, ie: Reverend, Doctor, Chairman, Senator, etc. It is important to him to have official recognition.

• Pride doesn't mind having his name exalted and, in fact, enjoys getting attention -- unless he thinks others know he enjoys attention, then he will not want to be exalted. (Others might reject him for being proud rather than admire him.)

• Pride loves to be in front of crowds. He enjoys the attention. (Pride hates to be in front of crowds. He is easily embarrassed.)

HUMILITY ASPIRES TO GLORIFY ONLY GOD

1. HUMILITY DRAWS ATTENTION TO GOD

Proverbs 27:2 Let another praise you, and not your own mouth; someone else, and not your own lips.

Jeremiah 9:23-24 This is what the LORD says: "Let not the wise man boast of his wisdom or the strong man boast of his strength or the rich man boast of his riches, 24 but let him who boasts boast about this: that he understands and knows me, that I am the LORD, who exercises kindness, justice and righteousness on earth, for in these I delight," declares the LORD.

2 Corinthians 10:17 But, "Let him who boasts boast in the Lord."

Galatians 6:14 May I never boast except in the cross of our Lord Jesus Christ, through which the world has been crucified to me, and I to the world.

James 4:16 As it is, you boast and brag. All such boasting is evil.

2 Corinthians 11:30 If I must boast, I will boast of the things that show my weakness.

2 Corinthians 12:9 But he said to me, "My grace is sufficient for you, for my power is made perfect in weakness." Therefore I will boast all the more gladly about my weaknesses, so that Christ's power may rest on me.

• Humility will seek for its name not to be exalted. It wants the Lord to be glorified.

• Humility sincerely takes no credit for accomplishments.

PRIDE ASPIRES TO BE GREAT!

2. PRIDE DRAWS ATTENTION TO ITSELF

Proverbs 10:18 He who conceals his hatred has lying lips, and whoever spreads slander is a fool.

Jeremiah 9:23-24 This is what the LORD says: "Let not the wise man boast of his wisdom or the strong man boast of his strength or the rich man boast of his riches, 24 but let him who boasts boast about this: that he understands and knows me, that I am the LORD, who exercises kindness, justice and righteousness on earth, for in these I delight," declares the LORD.

James 4:16 As it is, you boast and brag. All such boasting is evil.

Colossians 2:18 Do not let anyone who delights in false humility and the worship of angels disqualify you for the prize. Such a person goes into great detail about what he has seen, and his unspiritual mind puffs him up with idle notions.

• Pride boasts and brags.

• Pride offers his own credibility. He tries to show that what he has to say is worth listening to.

• Pride "spiritualizes" everything he says and does. He wants to be seen as "spiritual."

• Pride has the "Spiritual" answer, from the "godly" perspective, for every situation and conversation.

• Pride has a tendency to share with you what "spiritual" words or good advice he gave someone else.

• Pride can't wait to be the first to share news -- good or bad.

• Pride is a namedropper. He is a show-off.

• Pride lets filter into his conversations anything that might impress those who are listening.

• Pride says things "objectively" about himself, but which actually extol him. Attention is drawn to him rather than Jesus.

• Pride likes to present an image of himself and will have to bluff to uphold that image. (We may try to come across as godly, spiritual, cool, coy, smart, hip, suave, cute, funny, macho, shy, hard, cold, loving, tender, gentle, organized, intellectual, etc..)

HUMILITY ASPIRES TO GLORIFY ONLY GOD

2. HUMILITY DRAWS ATTENTION TO GOD

John 3:30 He must become greater; I must become less.

1 Corinthians 13:4 Love is patient, love is kind. It does not envy, it does not boast, it is not proud.

1 Corinthians 10:31 So whether you eat or drink or whatever you do, do it all for the glory of God.

1 Cor 11:1 Follow my example, as I follow the example of Christ.

- Humility is sincere.

- Humility is not interested in how others perceive him. He is interested in others.

- Humility doesn't put on a front.

- Humility is genuine.

- Humility is honest.

- Humility doesn't rely on outward success before others for self- acceptance. That is a by product of a right relationship with God.

PRIDE ASPIRES TO BE GREAT!

3. PRIDE STRIVES TO BE ADMIRED

Proverbs 29:25 Fear of man will prove to be a snare, but whoever trusts in the LORD is kept safe.

Matt 10:18 On my account you will be brought before governors and kings as witnesses to them and to the Gentiles.

John 12:43 for they loved praise from men more than praise from God.

James 3:14 But if you harbor bitter envy and selfish ambition in your hearts, do not boast about it or deny the truth.

1 Corinthians 5:2 And you are proud! Shouldn't you rather have been filled with grief and have put out of your fellowship the man who did this?

- Pride loves the approval of men.

- Pride is highly competitive. He must win!

- Pride hates to be a "loser." His successes determine his self-concept.

- Pride must speak about past sin with very little shame. He will try to glory in past carnality.

HUMILITY ASPIRES TO GLORIFY ONLY GOD

3. HUMILITY STRIVES TO PLEASE GOD

Eph 5:10 and find out what pleases the Lord.

2 Cor 5:9 So we make it our goal to please him, whether we are at home in the body or away from it.

1 Th 4:1 Finally, brothers, we instructed you how to live in order to please God, as in fact you are living. Now we ask you and urge you in the Lord Jesus to do this more and more.Gal 1:10 Am I now trying to win the approval of men, or of God? Or am I trying to please men? If I were still trying to please men, I would not be a servant of Christ.

- Humility puts to death the natural desires to impress other people and gain their acceptance or admiration.

- Humility has died to self. Humility doesn't talk much about himself.

PRIDE HAS AN OVER-EXALTED SELF VIEW

1. PRIDE BELIEVES HE IS GREAT

Ezekiel 28:5 By your great skill in trading you have increased your wealth, and because of your wealth your heart has grown proud.

Ezekiel 28:17 Your heart became proud on account of your beauty, and you corrupted your wisdom because of your splendor. So I threw you to the earth; I made a spectacle of you before kings.

Hosea 13:6 When I fed them, they were satisfied; when they were satisfied, they became proud; then they forgot me.

Proverbs 27:1 Do not boast about tomorrow, for you do not know what a day may bring forth.

• Pride consciously or subconsciously credits himself for all that he is or has.

• Pride has an over-developed sense of self-importance that causes him to expect or demand honor, respect, and special treatment.

• Pride is intolerant of anything or anyone that thwarts his will. He becomes indignant towards those who defy or frustrate him.

• Pride speaks in dogmatic terms: "I hate this..."; "I won't tolerate that..."; "I must have this..."; "I am right."

• Pride is the root of most anger. The greater the sense of self-importance the greater the offense. The greater the offense the more resentment and bitterness. Unforgiveness stems directly from pride.

• Pride is demanding and pushy.

• Pride is very anxious. He considers whatever he's doing to be of the highest importance.

• Pride is full of self-indulgence, therefore is impatient. He wants immediate gratification, and is intolerant of having to wait through unenjoyable experiences.

HUMILITY GIVES GOD THE CREDIT DUE HIM

1. HUMILITY BELIEVES ONLY GOD IS GREAT

Psalms 34:2 My soul will boast in the LORD; let the afflicted hear and rejoice.

1 Corinthians 1:28 He chose the lowly things of this world and the despised things--and the things that are not--to nullify the things that are,

James 1:17 Every good and perfect gift is from above, coming down from the Father of the heavenly lights, who does not change like shifting shadows.

Dan 2:21 He changes times and seasons; he sets up kings and deposes them. He gives wisdom to the wise and knowledge to the discerning.

Isa 40:23 He brings princes to naught and reduces the rulers of this world to nothing.

Isa 45:7 I form the light and create darkness, I bring prosperity and create disaster; I, the LORD, do all these things.

Rom 11:36 For from him and through him and to him are all things. To him be the glory forever! Amen.

Rom 15:15 I have written you quite boldly on some points, as if to remind you of them again, because of the grace God gave me 17 Therefore I glory in Christ Jesus in my service to God.

Ephesians 2:8-9 For it is by grace you have been saved, through faith--and this not from yourselves, it is the gift of God-- 9 not by works, so that no one can boast.

Rom 6:23 For the wages of sin is death, but the gift of God is eternal life in Christ Jesus our Lord.

Proverbs 16:32 Better a patient man than a warrior, a man who controls his temper than one who takes a city.

1 Corinthians 13:4 Love is patient, love is kind. It does not envy, it does not boast, it is not proud.

Ephesians 4:2 Be completely humble and gentle; be patient, bearing with one another in love.

James 1:2-4 Consider it pure joy, my brothers, whenever you face trials of many kinds, 3 because you know that the testing of your faith develops perseverance. 4 Perseverance must finish its work so that you may be mature and complete, not lacking anything.

James 5:10-11 Brothers, as an example of patience in the face of suffering, take the prophets who spoke in the name of the Lord. 11 As you know, we consider blessed those who have persevered. You have heard of Job's perseverance and have seen what the Lord finally brought about. The Lord is full of compassion and mercy.

1 Peter 2:23 When they hurled their insults at him, he did not retaliate; when he suffered, he made no threats. Instead, he entrusted himself to him who judges justly.

James 1:19 My dear brothers, take note of this: Everyone should be quick to listen, slow to speak and slow to become angry,

• Humility recognizes God as the source of all gifts, abilities and good fortune.

• Humility sees himself as a weak, fallible, human being who has been forgiven by a merciful God.

• Humility sees salvation as a free gift for which he wouldn't dream of taking credit.

• Humility does not demand his own way. He is patient.

• Humility willingly tolerates inconvenience and difficulties. In fact, his submission to trials makes him more godly.

• Humility is slow to anger. He doesn't hold a grudge, because he recognizes his own need for mercy.

PRIDE HAS AN OVER-EXALTED SELF VIEW

2. PRIDE LOVES TO TALK

Proverbs 15:2 The tongue of the wise commends knowledge, but the mouth of the fool gushes folly.

Proverbs 18:2 A fool finds no pleasure in understanding but delights in airing his own opinions.

Proverbs 20:3 It is to a man's honor to avoid strife, but every fool is quick to quarrel.

Proverbs 10:18-19 He who conceals his hatred has lying lips, and whoever spreads slander is a fool. 19 When words are many, sin is not absent, but he who holds his tongue is wise.

Proverbs 13:10 Pride only breeds quarrels, but wisdom is found in those who take advice.

Proverbs 17:19 He who loves a quarrel loves sin; he who builds a high gate invites destruction.

2 Timothy 2:23 Don't have anything to do with foolish and stupid arguments, because you know they produce quarrels.

Titus 3:9 But avoid foolish controversies and genealogies and arguments and quarrels about the law, because these are unprofitable and useless.

• Pride thinks what he has to say is very important.

• Pride views himself, his opinions, his experiences, and his insights as very necessary to be spoken.

• Pride will speak almost compulsively.

- Pride loves to demonstrate knowledge. Many spiritual and scriptural discussions can be a mere demonstration of knowledge. A compulsion to teach not driven by compassion finds its source in pride.

- Pride loves to acquire "knowledge." It is ammunition for debates and for showing off.

- Pride loves to "split-hairs," because it displays his "keen insights."

- Pride doesn't listen well. He always gets off the subject when he contributes to a discussion.

- Pride doesn't really interact with others in a discussion, but simply uses the subject being discussed as a platform from which to sermonize and voice his thoughts and opinions.

- Pride loves to debate and has very little love when doing so. Because so much of himself is invested in them his debates can easily become volatile.

HUMILITY GIVES GOD THE CREDIT DUE HIM

2. HUMILITY TALKS LITTLE

Proverbs 11:12 A man who lacks judgment derides his neighbor, but a man of understanding holds his tongue.

Proverbs 12:18 Reckless words pierce like a sword, but the tongue of the wise brings healing.

Proverbs 12:23 A prudent man keeps his knowledge to himself, but the heart of fools blurts out folly.

Proverbs 13:3 He who guards his lips guards his life, but he who speaks rashly will come to ruin.

Proverbs 17:27-28 A man of knowledge uses words with restraint, and a man of understanding is even-tempered. 28 Even a fool is thought wise if he keeps silent, and discerning if he holds his tongue.

James 1:19 My dear brothers, take note of this: Everyone should be quick to listen, slow to speak and slow to become angry,

• Humility is a very good listener.

• Humility is very wise.

• Humility doesn't talk a lot. in fact, he is hesitant to display his knowledge.

PRIDE HAS AN OVER-EXALTED SELF VIEW

3. PRIDE IS UNTEACHABLE

Proverbs 3:7 Do not be wise in your own eyes; fear the LORD and shun evil.

Proverbs 9:8 Do not rebuke a mocker or he will hate you; rebuke a wise man and he will love you.

Proverbs 26:12 Do you see a man wise in his own eyes? There is more hope for a fool than for him.

Proverbs 28:26 He who trusts in himself is a fool, but he who walks in wisdom is kept safe.

1 Corinthians 3:18-21 Do not deceive yourselves. If any one of you thinks he is wise by the standards of this age, he should become a "fool" so that he may become wise. 19 For the wisdom of this world is foolishness in God's sight. As it is written: "He catches the wise in their craftiness"; 20 and again, "The Lord knows that the thoughts of the wise are futile." 21 So then, no more boasting about men! All things are yours,

Galatians 6:3-4 If anyone thinks he is something when he is nothing, he deceives himself. 4 Each one should test his own actions. Then he can take pride in himself, without comparing himself to somebody else,

Isaiah 5:21 Woe to those who are wise in their own eyes and clever in their own sight.

1 Corinthians 8:2 The man who thinks he knows something does not yet know as he ought to know.

Proverbs 18:13 He who answers before listening -- that is his folly and his shame.

• Pride is a know-it-all. He thinks he is smarter than he actually is.

• Pride will always instruct others and rarely is open for real learning from them.

• Pride views himself very highly. He may tend to think of himself as having some kind of special authority, gift, or knowledge.

• Pride tends to say, "I know," a lot when listening to another's statements. He doesn't want them to think there is something he doesn't know.

• When pride asks a question seeking help with a problem, he frequently offers a solution simultaneously so as not to appear completely ignorant.

• Pride is not usually a very good listener. He's more interested in talking than listening. Consequently, pride is very impatient in conversation. He interrupts a lot.

• When asked a question, pride always feels like he has to have the answer. It's not easy for him to say, "I don't know."

• Pride is stubborn and inflexible. His self-confidence hinders his growth.

HUMILITY GIVES GOD THE CREDIT DUE HIM

3. HUMILITY IS EASILY TAUGHT

Proverbs 19:20 Listen to advice and accept instruction, and in the end you will be wise.

Proverbs 13:10 Pride only breeds quarrels, but wisdom is found in those who take advice.

Proverbs 15:31 He who listens to a life-giving rebuke will be at home among the wise.

1 Corinthians 13:4 Love is patient, love is kind. It does not envy, it does not boast, it is not proud.

• Humility can keep his mouth shut even when he's being told something he already knows.

• Humility is secure. He doesn't have to prove anything.

• Humility, in fact, is not afraid to learn something from someone who knows very little. He loves truth no matter how young or how proud the source from which it comes.

• Humility is meek. He doesn't usually interrupt unless it's for the other's good. He's patient.

PRIDE HAS AN OVER-EXALTED SELF VIEW

4. PRIDE IDOLIZES HIMSELF

Psalms 10:4 In his pride the wicked does not seek him; in all his thoughts there is no room for God.

Isaiah 47:10 You have trusted in your wickedness and have said, 'No one sees me.' Your wisdom and knowledge mislead you when you say to yourself, 'I am, and there is none besides me.'

Hosea 10:13 But you have planted wickedness, you have reaped evil, you have eaten the fruit of deception. Because you have depended on your own strength and on your many warriors,

1 Corinthians 10:12 So, if you think you are standing firm, be careful that you don't fall!

Philippians 2:14 Do everything without complaining or arguing,

• Pride is full of self-confidence. He thinks that within himself he has the ability to do anything.

• Pride lives not for God, but for himself. His plans, his wishes, his will is supreme and sought before all else.

• Pride is full of himself. He is self-sufficient.

• Pride thinks he deserves respect and love from others and a trouble-free life from God. He feels like everyone owes him. Pride is therefore unappreciative and ungrateful. He is rarely satisfied.

• Pride is clueless to his debt to God. Pride gets angry at God.

HUMILITY GIVES GOD THE CREDIT DUE HIM

4. HUMILITY UNDERSTANDS ITS INDEBTEDNESS TO GOD

1 Samuel 17:37 The LORD who delivered me from the paw of the lion and the paw of the bear will deliver me from the hand of this Philistine." Saul said to David, "Go, and the LORD be with you."

2 Corinthians 5:15 And he died for all, that those who live should no longer live for themselves but for him who died for them and was raised again.

Ephesians 6:19-20 Pray also for me, that whenever I open my mouth, words may be given me so that I will fearlessly make known the mystery of the gospel, 20 for which I am an ambassador in chains. Pray that I may declare it fearlessly, as I should.

• Humility trusts in God for his abilities -- not in himself.

• Humility knows he deserves only Hell and judgment so accepts life's difficulties.

• Humility is more than willing to accept responsibility for his actions.

PRIDE HAS AN OVER-EXALTED SELF VIEW

5. PRIDE LOVES POWER

3 John 1:9 I wrote to the church, but Diotrephes, who loves to be first, will have nothing to do with us.

• Pride finds gratification in having authority over people. Controlling others and their lives reinforces his sense of importance.

• Pride loves to have control of people and events -- not just for the feeling of power, but also for selfishness. With control of things around him he is assured of his personal plans being accomplished. Pride likes to have his way.

HUMILITY GIVES GOD THE CREDIT DUE HIM

5. HUMILITY YIELDS POWER

• Humility accepts authority, but gains nothing from those under his supervision.

• Humility has submitted itself to God's rule so welcomes whatever He decides to allow. His peace is not dependent on everyone and everything going his way.

• Humility has no need to be "in charge."

PRIDE IS SELF-RIGHTEOUS

1. PRIDE IS CONDESCENDING

Romans 11:20 Granted. But they were broken off because of unbelief, and you stand by faith. Do not be arrogant, but be afraid.

Ezekiel 16:49 "'Now this was the sin of your sister Sodom: She and her daughters were arrogant, overfed and unconcerned; they did not help the poor and needy.

1 Corinthians 4:6 Now, brothers, I have applied these things to myself and Apollos for your benefit, so that you may learn from us the meaning of the saying, "Do not go beyond what is written." Then you will not take pride in one man over against another.

1 John 1:8 If we claim to be without sin, we deceive ourselves and the truth is not in us. 10 If we claim we have not sinned, we make him out to be a liar and his word has no place in our lives.

Romans 10:1-4 Brothers, my heart's desire and prayer to God for the Israelites is that they may be saved. 2 For I can testify about them that they are zealous for God, but their zeal is not based on knowledge. 3 Since they did not know the righteousness that comes from God and sought to establish their own, they did not submit to God's righteousness. 4 Christ is the end of the law so that there may be righteousness for everyone who believes.

• Pride is arrogant. He condescends to others.

• Pride sees many people who are not worth his time.

• Pride does not often pray for those perceived as less spiritual.

• Pride actually thinks he is a little better than others.

• Pride says "I do not sin."

• Pride professes "salvation by grace," but subconsciously credits himself with his right-standing with God, thereby resulting in an elevated platform from which to look down on others.

HUMILITY DEPENDS ON CHRIST'S RIGHTEOUSNESS

1. HUMILITY SEES OTHERS AS EQUALS

Gal 3:28 There is neither Jew nor Greek, slave nor free, male nor female, for you are all one in Christ Jesus.

Romans 12:16 Live in harmony with one another. Do not be proud, but be willing to associate with people of low position. Do not be conceited.

Philippians 2:3-4 Do nothing out of selfish ambition or vain conceit, but in humility consider others better than yourselves. 4 Each of you should look not only to your own interests, but also to the interests of others.

• Humility sees others as his equals, no matter what their position in life. When given authority he still serves those under his care.

• Humility sees all people as worth his time.

• Humility prays for anyone, no matter what their spiritual level of growth.

• Humility esteems others as better than himself.

• Humility properly hates his sin, but readily submits to God's mercy and grace. He doesn't try to atone for his sins by preoccupying himself with his failures and mistakes

PRIDE IS SELF-RIGHTEOUS

2. PRIDE IS EXCLUSIVE

2 Corinthians 12:20 For I am afraid that when I come I may not find you as I want you to be, and you may not find me as you want me to be. I fear that there may be quarreling, jealousy, outbursts of anger, factions, slander, gossip, arrogance and disorder.

1 Corinthians 1:10-13 I appeal to you, brothers, in the name of our Lord Jesus Christ, that all of you agree with one another so that there may be no divisions among you and that you may be perfectly united in mind and thought. 11 My brothers, some from Chloe's household have informed me that there are quarrels among you. 12 What I mean is this: One of you says, "I follow Paul"; another, "I follow Apollos"; another, "I follow Cephas "; still another, "I follow Christ." 13 Is

Christ divided? Was Paul crucified for you? Were you baptized into the name of Paul?

1 Corinthians 3:3-4 You are still worldly. For since there is jealousy and quarreling among you, are you not worldly? Are you not acting like mere men? 4 For when one says, "I follow Paul," and another, "I follow Apollos," are you not mere men?

• Pride loves to feel like it has cornered the market on Truth.

• Pride loves to "pity" those less enlightened.

HUMILITY DEPENDS ON CHRIST'S RIGHTEOUSNESS

2. HUMILITY CRAVES UNITY

Ephesians 4:3 Make every effort to keep the unity of the Spirit through the bond of peace.

Colossians 2:2 My purpose is that they may be encouraged in heart and united in love, so that they may have the full riches of complete understanding, in order that they may know the mystery of God, namely, Christ,

1 Peter 3:8 Finally, all of you, live in harmony with one another; be sympathetic, love as brothers, be compassionate and humble.

• Humility may have more "light" than others, but doesn't use it as an excuse to separate himself from those not yet enlightened.

• Humility values unity of spirit more than agreement on peripheral doctrinal issues.

PRIDE IS SELF-RIGHTEOUS

3. PRIDE IS CRITICAL

Psalms 123:4 We have endured much ridicule from the proud, much contempt from the arrogant.

Proverbs 21:24 The proud and arrogant man--" Mocker" is his name; he behaves with overweening pride.

Proverbs 12:16 A fool shows his annoyance at once, but a prudent man overlooks an insult.

James 4:11-12 Brothers, do not slander one another. Anyone who speaks against his brother or judges him speaks against the law and judges it. When you judge the law, you are not keeping it, but sitting in judgment on it. 12 There is only one Lawgiver and Judge, the one who is able to save and destroy. But you--who are you to judge your neighbor?

James 5:9 Don't grumble against each other, brothers, or you will be judged. The Judge is standing at the door!

Romans 14:4 Who are you to judge someone else's servant? To his own master he stands or falls. And he will stand, for the Lord is able to make him stand. 10 You, then, why do you judge your brother? Or why do you look down on your brother? For we will all stand before God's judgment seat. 13 Therefore let us stop passing judgment on one another. Instead, make up your mind not to put any stumbling block or obstacle in your brother's way.

• Pride is very critical of others. He always finds fault with everything. He has little mercy.

• Pride delights in his ability to point out error. He doesn't hesitate to express someone or something's shortcomings.

• Pride usually expresses little concern when he is mentioning someones shortcomings. Even if concern is expressed, it's tagged on as only an afterthought so as not to appear self-righteous.

• Pride is legalistic. He creates extra-biblical rules and standards by which he judges himself and others.

• Pride can be quite snobbish. Scorning and scoffing are common attitudes. Disdain is frequently heard in his voice.

• Pride's conversations reveal little constructive criticism, but rather sarcastic cuts and jabs.

• Pride tears down. He has fun at others expense.

HUMILITY DEPENDS ON CHRIST'S RIGHTEOUSNESS

3. HUMILITY THINKS THE BEST OF OTHERS

Galatians 6:1 Brothers, if someone is caught in a sin, you who are spiritual should restore him gently. But watch yourself, or you also may be tempted.

Proverbs 15:1 A gentle answer turns away wrath, but a harsh word stirs up anger.

Proverbs 17:9 He who covers over an offense promotes love, but whoever repeats the matter separates close friends.

Proverbs 19:11 A man's wisdom gives him patience; it is to his glory to overlook an offense.

Proverbs 12:16 A fool shows his annoyance at once, but a prudent man overlooks an insult.

1 Corinthians 13:7 It always protects, always trusts, always hopes, always perseveres.

• Humility is discerning, but not critical.

• Humility is firm, but not harsh.

• Humility might recognize another's shortcomings, but will preserve their reputation, not destroy it.

• Humility will find something positive to say when all others are tempted to only criticize.

• Humility is understanding. It is full of mercy towards others.

• Humility gives sincere, concerned reproof, rather than off-the-cuff sarcastic cuts.

PRIDE IS SELF-RIGHTEOUS

4. PRIDE IS JUDGMENTAL

Colossians 2:16 Therefore do not let anyone judge you by what you eat or drink, or with regard to a religious festival, a New Moon celebration or a Sabbath day.

1 Corinthians 4:5 Therefore judge nothing before the appointed time; wait till the Lord comes. He will bring to light what is hidden in darkness and will expose the motives of men's hearts. At that time each will receive his praise from God.

1 Corinthians 13:6 Love does not delight in evil but rejoices with the truth.

• Pride quickly senses pride in another.

• Pride is especially quick to judge the pride in another man's heart.

• Pride frequently wants to see another man humbled and knocked off his "high-horse."

HUMILITY DEPENDS ON CHRIST'S RIGHTEOUSNESS

4. HUMILITY IS MERCIFUL

Matthew 5:44-45 But I tell you: Love your enemies and pray for those who persecute you, 45 that you may be sons of your Father in heaven. He causes his sun to rise on the evil and the good, and sends rain on the righteous and the unrighteous. 48 Be perfect, therefore, as your heavenly Father is perfect.

Matthew 18:33 Shouldn't you have had mercy on your fellow servant just as I had on you?'

Luke 6:36 Be merciful, just as your Father is merciful.

Ephesians 5:32 This is a profound mystery--but I am talking about Christ and the church.

Colossians 3:13 Bear with each other and forgive whatever grievances you may have against one another. Forgive as the Lord forgave you.

• Humility may recognize pride in someone else, but compassion is evoked - not disdain.

• Humility gives mercy to the proud, because Humility realizes that he himself has pride...and God has been merciful to him. The fruit of mercy is mercy.

FINAL THOUGHTS ON HUMILITY

❖ Humility will probably always see pride in his life. Does a humble person say to himself, "Gee, I'm humble,"?

❖ A proud person will take pride in being humble and meek, but a humble person will be humbled by his pride.

❖ Pride delights in recognizing itself. Though pride won't want to see itself, once it does, it wants to impress others with its insight and humility. It wants to impress others that it's insightful enough to make that last statement. It even wants to impress others with its ability to recognize itself at all levels - even in making this very statement. It even wants others to be impressed with its wit to make this whole point. Pride is deceitful and disgusting!

❖ We are no shock to God. He knows our hearts far better than we do even now, but He still loves us. He has chosen to store His treasures in clay vessels.

HOW CAN WE GROW IN HUMILITY?

1. We must starve pride.

Matthew 16:24 Then Jesus said to his disciples, "If anyone would come after me, he must deny himself and take up his cross and follow me.

Romans 8:13 For if you live according to the sinful nature, you will die; but if by the Spirit you put to death the misdeeds of the body, you will live,

Colossians 3:5 Put to death, therefore, whatever belongs to your earthly nature: sexual immorality, impurity, lust, evil desires and greed, which is idolatry.

2. We must see our weakness.

2 Corinthians 11:30 If I must boast, I will boast of the things that show my weakness.

2 Corinthians 12:5 I will boast about a man like that, but I will not boast about myself, except about my weaknesses. 9 But he said to me, "My grace is sufficient for you, for my power is made perfect in weakness." Therefore I will boast all the more gladly about my weaknesses, so that Christ's power may rest on me. 10 That is why, for Christ's sake, I delight in weaknesses, in insults, in hardships, in persecutions, in difficulties. For when I am weak, then I am strong. 11 I have made a fool of myself, but you drove me to it. I ought to have been commended by you, for I am not in the least inferior to the "super-apostles," even though I am nothing.

3. We must see God.

Job 42:5 My ears had heard of you but now my eyes have seen you.

Isaiah 6:5 "Woe to me!" I cried. "I am ruined! For I am a man of unclean lips, and I live among a people of unclean lips, and my eyes have seen the King, the LORD Almighty."

Numbers 12:3 (Now Moses was a very humble man, more humble than anyone else on the face of the earth.)

Deuteronomy 34:10-12 Since then, no prophet has risen in Israel like Moses, whom the LORD knew face to face, 11 who did all those miraculous signs and wonders the LORD sent him to do in Egypt--to Pharaoh and to all his officials and to his whole land. 12 For no one has ever shown the mighty power or performed the awesome deeds that Moses did in the sight of all Israel.

For those who want more understanding and help applying what they have learned in this book, I recommend the seminar for which this syllabus was prepared:

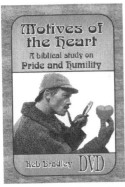

Motives of the Heart
A biblical study in pride and humility

Although originally presented as part of a pastors training course, all believers will find great value in this biblical study in pride and humility. Particularly valuable for the mature Christian who is ready to peel back the layers of his heart and see himself as God does.

"DRAMATICALLY LIFE-CHANGING" is how most people describe this seminar. It is the only set we offer that comes with a warning: *This message may have serious humbling effects on the listener!*

Available in a 3-disc CD set and a 6 session DVD set.

For these materials or dozens of more titles, contact your source for this book, or request a complete catalog from
Family Ministries   800-545-1729
www.familyministries.com

More materials by Reb Bradley

Powerful Christian Living: *Following Jesus into Wholeness.* Amazing series revealing Jesus' path to Christian maturity – *12 CD set*

Breaking Free*: Escaping an Exclusive Christian Group, book*

FIG LEAVES: *Exposing hindrances to successful repentance* -- Reb, as an instructor of Biblical Counseling, documents the defense mechanisms we use to avoid taking personal responsibility; *booklet*

Managing the Mouth: *Victory over complaining, arguing, gossip, and other poisons of the tongue; 4-CDs*

The Power of Love: A powerful and refreshing look at the true nature of love, and the effect it has on those who give and receive it. 6-CD set

Happiness in Marriage: *Discovering the blessing God intended* – 5-disc DVD set with 2 syllabi.

Help for the Struggling Marriage: What the Bible says about ending marriage by divorce – book

Reconciling With Your Wife: Critical help for the husband who finds himself abandoned by his wife – *book*

Influencing Children's Hearts – 4-CD set

Child Training Tips: *What I wish I knew when my children were young – book*

Biblical Insights into Child Training Establishing control in the home and raising godly children – *8 CD/DVD set*

For these materials or dozens of more titles, contact your source for this book, or request a complete catalog from
Family Ministries   800-545-1729
www.familyministries.com

41633736R00032

Made in the USA
Lexington, KY
21 May 2015